Helping Children See Jesus

ISBN: 978-1-64104-006-8

The Tabernacle Part 2
A Picture of the Lord Jesus
Old Testament Volume 10:
Exodus Part 5

Author: Arlene Piepgrass and Katherine E. Hershey
Illustrator: Vernon Henkel
Computer Graphic Artist: Yuko Willoughby
Typesetting and Layout: Morgan Melton, Patricia Pope

© 2018 Bible Visuals International
PO Box 153, Akron, PA 17501-0153
Phone: (717) 859-1131
www.biblevisuals.org

All rights reserved. No part of this publication may be reproduced, stored in a retrieval system or transmitted in any form by any means, electronic, mechanical, photocopy, recording or otherwise, without the prior permission of the publisher, except as provided by USA copyright law.

RELATED ITEMS

To access related items (such as activities, memory verse posters and translated texts) please visit our web store at shop.biblevisuals.org and enter 2010 in the search box on the page.

FREE TEXT DOWNLOAD

To access a FREE printable copy of the teaching text (PDF format) in English or other available languages, enter S2010DL in the search box. Add the item to your cart, and use coupon code XTACSV17 at checkout. Once your order is processed you will receive an email with a link to the free download.

Look unto Me, and be ye saved, all the ends of the earth; for I am God, and there is none else.

Isaiah 45:22

And what agreement hath the temple of God with idols? For ye are the temple of the living God.
2 Corinthians 6:16a

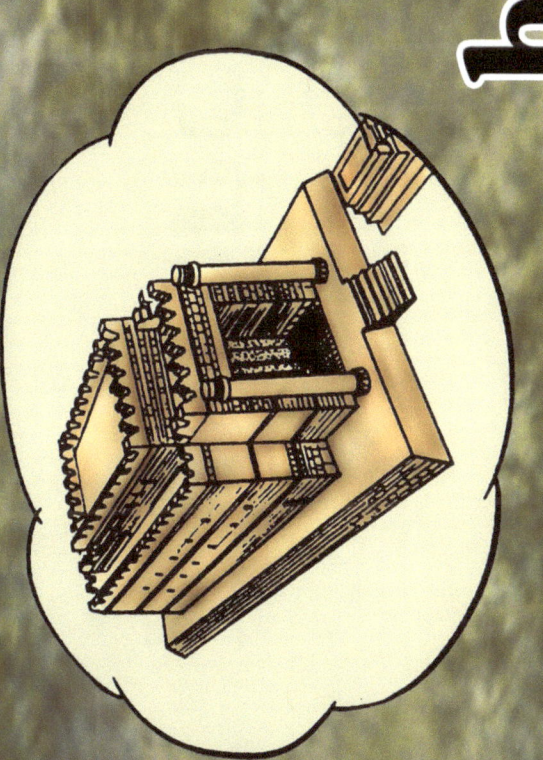

"For Christ is not entered into the holy places made with hands, which are the figures of the true; but into Heaven itself, now to appear in the presence of God for us."

Hebrews 9:24

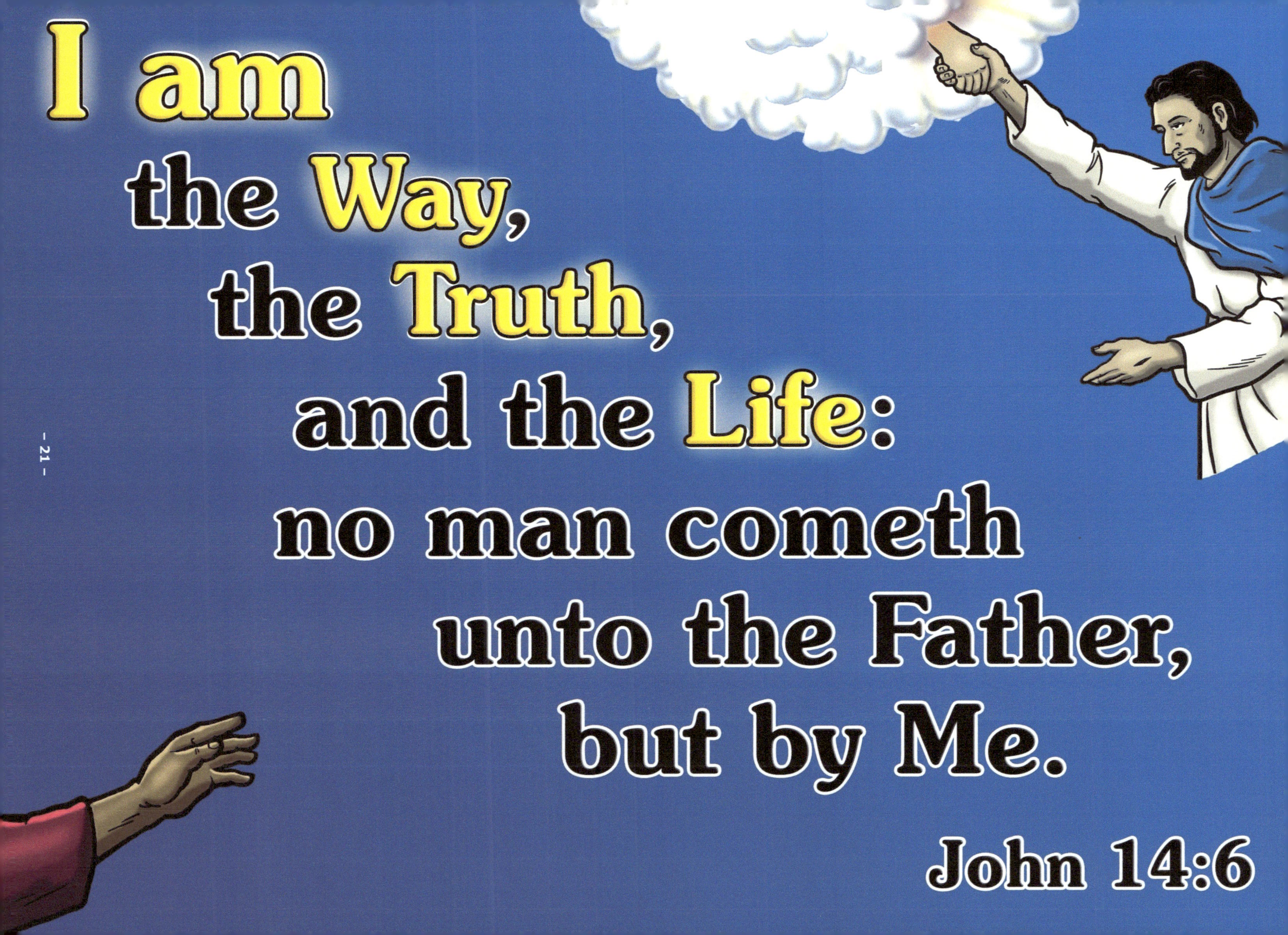

I am the Way, the Truth, and the Life: no man cometh unto the Father, but by Me. John 14:6

Lesson 1
THE TABERNACLE COVERINGS

NOTE TO THE TEACHER

If possible, have your students make a reproduction of the Tabernacle. Each one in the class could be responsible for one of the furnishings, a few pillars, one of the coverings or curtains. Determine the size of your Tabernacle by the number in your group. All should be able to see each object. Discuss the typical significance of each piece with the person making it. Doing this project during class time is well worthwhile since students usually remember about 90% of what they hear, see and *do*. In contrast, they may remember about 10% of what they *hear* only!

The Tabernacle teaches that God is absolutely holy. (The walls shut GOD *in*, Exodus 25:22.) It teaches the utter sinfulness of mankind. (The walls shut THEM *out*, Numbers 3:10.) And it teaches the ONLY way of man's approach to God (that is, through BLOOD, Hebrews 9:22).

If you elect to teach only one of the memory verses for the entire volume, we suggest using John 14:6. Please make certain that your students understand that the story part of our lessons is imaginary. But the facts are absolutely true.

Using the illustrations, review previous lessons thoroughly. This is extremely important!

THE HOLY PLACE

It is difficult to imagine the awe with which the priests served the Lord inside the Holy Place. It was a serious matter to be a mediator–going between God and man. Service in the Tabernacle was to be conducted exactly as God had commanded. Disobedience meant death! (See Leviticus 10:1-5.)

Just as the worship was ordered by God, so the Tabernacle itself was designed by Him. He told Moses, "Speak unto the children of Israel, that they bring Me an offering: of every man who gives it willingly with his heart you shall take My offering . . . And let them make Me a sanctuary, that I may dwell among them. According to all that I show you, after the pattern of the Tabernacle, and the pattern of all the furnishings thereof, even so shall you make it." (See Exodus 25:1-9.)

To make certain that all was done according to His specifications, God appointed two men to be in charge of building the Tabernacle. "And Moses called Bezaleel and Aholiab, and every wisehearted man, in whose heart the Lord had put wisdom, even every one whose heart stirred him to come unto the work to do it . . . And all the wise men, that wrought all the work of the sanctuary, came every man from his work which he made." (See Exodus 35:30-36:7; 31:1-11.)

From the book of Hebrews we learn why everything was done with such perfect exactness. The Tabernacle, its furnishings, its ceremonies, were illustrations of the person and work of the Lord Jesus Christ, given hundreds of years before He came to earth!

"Oh, the depth of the riches both of the wisdom and knowledge of God! How unsearchable are His judgments, and His ways past finding out!" (Romans 11:33)

Scripture to be studied: Exodus 26:1-37; 36:8-36; Leviticus 16:5-10, 21-22; Hebrews 7:23-10:22

The *aim* of the lesson: To show the exactness with which God designed the Tabernacle.

What your students should *know*: The Tabernacle revealed Christ and His ministry hundreds of years before He came to earth.

What your students should *feel*: A desire to have a close personal relationship with Christ (in contrast to knowing about Him).

What your students should *do*:
Unsaved: Receive the Lord Jesus as Saviour from sin.
Saved: Purpose to know Christ better by studying the Word of God.

Lesson outline (for the teacher's and students' notebooks):

1. The Tabernacle–from the outside (Exodus 26:1-6, 36-37; 36:8-13).
2. Inside the Tabernacle (Exodus 26:15-29; 36:20-36).
3. The coverings of the Tabernacle (Exodus 26:7-14; 36:14-19; Leviticus 16:5-10, 21-22).
4. The coverings–reminders of the Lord Jesus.

The verse to be memorized:

Look unto Me, and be ye saved, all the ends of the earth; for I am God, and there is none else. (Isaiah 45:22)

REVIEW

In the first of these lessons on the Tabernacle, we learned of the curtain around the court. Also, we saw the one way of entrance–the gate. In the second lesson we saw what was inside the court.

1. What piece of furniture was just inside the curtain? *(The brazen–or bronze–altar)*
2. Why was it called "the bronze altar"? *(It was covered with bronze.)*
3. What was under the bronze? *(Acacia wood)*
4. How did the wood and bronze picture the Lord Jesus? *(The wood is a reminder that the Lord Jesus, God the Son, became a man. The bronze reminds us that He is strong. He never changes His mind about sin–He always hates it.)*
5. Why is the lamb a reminder of the Lord Jesus Christ? *(He is the Lamb of God who died for the sin of the world.)*
6. Although the animal offerings were a reminder of Christ's death on the cross, what was the distinctive difference? *(The animal offerings were repeated again and again. Christ's offering was a once for all sacrifice for sin.)*
7. What else was inside the court? *(The laver and its foot)* For what purpose was the laver and its foot used? *(The priests washed their hands and feet there.)* What was used for making the laver and its foot? *(Polished mirrors)*
8. Why does the laver remind us of the Lord Jesus Christ? *(When we look into the mirror–the perfect life of the Lord Jesus–we see how sinful we are.)*
9. What does the washing at the laver mean to us? *(After we are born into the family of God, we may–and do–sin. These sins need to be confessed to God so we may be cleansed.)*

(Teacher: Some of these questions will call for rather detailed answers. But do review, praying that the students will absorb these wonderful truths.)

THE LESSON

Phinehas was hungry. His mouth watered as he smelled the good food his mother was cooking at their tent. "When will Father get home?" he asked.

"Soon," his mother answered, smiling. "Then we can eat."

"Mother, are you glad Father is a priest?" Phinehas wanted to know.

"Oh, yes, Phinehas! It is a great honor for him to serve the living and true God. I am delighted that he is a priest."

"I, too, am glad," Phinehas declared. "He answers all my questions about the Tabernacle." Wrinkling his forehead, he added, "The Tabernacle does not look very nice on the outside does it, Mother?"

1. THE TABERNACLE—FROM THE OUTSIDE
Exodus 26:1-6; 36-37; 36:8-13

Mother shook her head. "No, it does not. The *outside* is not beautiful. But your father can tell us about the *inside* and that must be wonderful to see."

Show Illustration #1

Later, as they ate their evening meal, Father told them about it. "The curtain at the door of the Tabernacle is much like the curtain at the gate to the court," he explained. "It hangs from five pillars which are overlaid with gold."

Phinehas nodded his head. "I know, Father. The pillars covered with gold are magnificent. I can see them from the gate."

2. INSIDE THE TABERNACLE
Exodus 26:15-29; 36:20-36

Show Illustration #2

Eleazar spoke again: "The tabernacle is divided into two sections. A thick, heavy curtain, called *the veil*, separates the two rooms. Like the curtain over the ceiling, the veil is embroidered with cherubim. The walls of the Tabernacle are gold-covered boards. They are fastened together outside with bars which fit through golden rings. Remember, Phinehas, gold always reminds us of God and His righteous glory."

Here is another truth to be learned. The Bible teaches that those whose trust is in the Lord Jesus are "hid with Christ in God." So the gold-covered boards speak of believers hidden away in the righteousness of God. Remember: these were *individual* boards. But they were held together by bars to make one building. So Christ makes all who have trusted in Him *one*: one body, one building, one Church. (See 1 Corinthians 12:12-13; Ephesians 1:22-23; 2:19-22; 5:30.) The Tabernacle was God's special dwelling place. Just so, all believers in Christ are the dwelling place of God. (See 1 Corinthians 6:19-20.)

Eleazar explained to his son how the boards were kept in place: "The gold-covered boards rest in sockets made of silver."

In that day, much of the money was silver. Silver was used to pay the price of an object. Often when the Bible speaks of *paying a price*, it uses the word "redeemed." For example, "You were not redeemed with . . . silver . . . but with the precious blood of Christ" (1 Peter 1:18-19). The Tabernacle sockets cost about $170,000 in our money. What a price! But the Lord Jesus Christ paid much, much more for us. He gave His life and bought us with His own precious blood.

The boards rested in silver sockets. Christian believers rest in the Lord Jesus who paid with His blood for the sins of the world.

3. THE COVERINGS OF THE TABERNACLE
Exodus 26:7-14; 36:14-19; Leviticus 16:5-10, 21-22

Now let us listen again to Phinehas as he talks to his father. "Mother and I were talking about the outside covering of the Tabernacle. It is not pretty, is it?"

"No, my son, it is not. But it is strong because it is made of badgers' skins. This badger skin covering protects the Tabernacle from the weather."

Phinehas remembered his shoes were also made of badgers' skins. They too were strong and protected his feet.

Are you ready for another reminder of the Lord Jesus? The Bible says, "There is no beauty that we should desire Him" (Isaiah 53:2). He looked like an ordinary man when He lived here on earth. People did not come to the Lord Jesus because of His looks. But oh, how wonderful He is! And strong. He cares for and protects His own day by day.

Phinehas and his father discussed the other coverings. The one underneath the badgers' skins was made of rams' skins dyed red. "Rams are used for sacrifices," Eleazar reminded his son.

Phinehas nodded his head. "I know," he said. "And the red cover reminds us of the sacrifice which dies in place of the sinner." (This likeness to the Lord Jesus is so clear that it may not need an explanation.)

Phinehas announced, "I can see the next covering from the gate. Part of it hangs over the front of the curtain at the door of the Tabernacle."

"Yes, Phinehas, and that covering is made of goats' hair," Eleazar explained.

Show Illustration #3

Father continued, "Two goats are used each year on the Day of Atonement. The high priest places his hand on the head of one of the goats while the sins of the people are confessed. That goat is killed and sacrificed on the altar. The priest then lays his hands on the head of the other goat. Again he confesses the people's sins. The second goat is then taken into the wilderness and deliberately lost and forgotten forever. God *covers* our sons with the blood of the sacrifice. He also *forgets* those sins."

Phinehas listened carefully to all of this. The goats' hair covering hanging over the front of the Tabernacle (see Illustration #1) would always remind him that God covers sins and forgets them.

Eleazar added, "The fourth covering, the one inside, is the loveliest of all. Few have seen that covering."

Phinehas knew the reason for this. It could only be seen inside the Tabernacle. And no one except the priests could enter the Tabernacle.

Show Illustration #4

– 23 –

Father explained, "This beautiful covering is actually the ceiling of the Tabernacle. It is something like the curtain at the gate–only much more beautiful. Blue, purple and scarlet are woven into the fine white linen. Figures of cherubim are embroidered into it."

(Phinehas knew that cherubim were angels. He remembered that Adam and Eve were forced out of the Garden of Eden when they sinned. The cherubim were placed at the gate to keep them from reentering.)

Eleazar explained, "This covering is made of ten separate curtains. They are fastened together with golden clasps." Phinehas closed his eyes tightly and tried to imagine exactly what it was like–the blue, purple and scarlet, the embroidered cherubim and clasps of gold. He thought of the other coverings, too.

4. THE COVERINGS– REMINDERS OF THE LORD JESUS

While Phinehas is thinking about the four coverings, would you like to think about the Lord Jesus? Some people think of Him simply as another man. To them, He is not at all attractive. He is like the outside badger skin covering of the Tabernacle.

To others, the Lord Jesus is the One who died as a sacrifice for sin. They know this to be true. But they have never received Him as the One who died for *their* sins. The second covering of rams' skins dyed red reminds them that Jesus died–that is all.

Then there are those who *have* received the Lord Jesus as their Saviour. They have been cleansed from sin through His blood. The goats' hair covering is a reminder to them that Christ gave His life when He died in their place.

There are still others who, having trusted in Christ as Saviour, are eager to know Him better. They read God's Word each day. They spend time with Him in prayer. They tell others of Him. They attend church and Sunday school to learn even more about Him. They obey Him. They trust Him to guide their lives. Such people have seen the loveliness of the Lord Jesus. These understand the meaning of the inside covering of the Tabernacle.

Everyone today fits into one of these four groups. Which group are *you* in?

Lesson 2
THE HOLY PLACE

Scripture to be studied: Exodus 25:23-39; 26:31-35; 30:1-8; 36:35-36; 37:10-28; John 6:35; 8:12; Hebrews 7:25

The *aim* of the lesson: To show that the objects in the Holy Place typify Christ and His activities for His own.

What your students should *know*: That the Lord Jesus Christ is the believer's light, food and intercessor.

What your students should *feel*: A desire for greater knowledge of this all-sufficient Lord.

What your students should *do*: Follow the "Light of the world"; feed on the "Bread of life" through the Word; fully trust the One who prays for them.

Lesson outline (for the teacher's and students' notebooks):

1. The Veil (Exodus 26:31-35; 36:35-36).
2. The Table of Showbread (Exodus 25:23-30; 37:10-16; John 6:35).
3. The Lampstand (Exodus 25:31-39; 37:17-24; John 8:12).
4. The Altar of Incense (Exodus 30:1-8; 37:25-28; Hebrews 7:25).

The verse to be memorized:

And what agreement hath the temple of God with idols? For ye are the temple of the living God. (2 Corinthians 6:16a)

THE LESSON

Phinehas sat near the gate of the Tabernacle. He was not alone on this day. Several friends were with him. They talked of many things–the hard work they had done in Egypt and the cruel treatment they received from the Egyptians. They spoke of the Passover night. They discussed God's amazing deliverance at the Red Sea. Finally, they talked about the Tabernacle.

"Phinehas, you ought to know a lot about the Tabernacle. Your father is a priest. The priests can even enter inside the tent. Please tell us about it," one boy begged.

"I can tell you some of the things," Phinehas answered. "I have asked my father lots of questions."

"What is it like inside the curtain at the door? I have heard there are two rooms," said another.

"Yes," Phinehas nodded. "There are two rooms. The first room–the one just inside the curtain–is called *the Holy Place*.

NOTE TO THE TEACHER

The study of Biblical typology is important and profitable. The Apostle Paul, when recording certain historical events, wrote, ". . . these things happened to them for examples (or, *types*), and they are written for our admonition" (1 Corinthians 10:11). The types keep us from making the mistakes others made. They teach us spiritual truths and spiritual lessons. (See Romans 15:4.).

Types are *primarily* connected with Christ and truths which center around Him. (See 1 Corinthians 10:4.) The reason for considering the Tabernacle as a type is given in Hebrews 9. It is important to observe that it is a pattern (or miniature) of the "true Tabernacle" in Heaven itself. (See Hebrews 8:2; 9:24.)

Review types from all the previous lessons. Particularly emphasize the colors and metals, since these are repeated in several places throughout the Tabernacle. Questions should include the gold-covered boards and each of the coverings in their relation to Christ. It is good for the students to know what the coverings were. It is much more important for them to know the *meanings* of the coverings.

That room is larger than the other. At the back of the Holy Place there is a magnificent, thick curtain called the 'veil.'"

1. THE VEIL
Exodus 26:31-35; 36:35-36

"What is the veil like?" the others chorused.

Show Illustration #5

"It is something like the curtains at the gate and the door, only much more beautiful. It is similar to the inside covering over the top of the Tabernacle– except it is made of one piece."

Phinehas thought that his friends did not know much about the veil. Their fathers had never been inside the tabernacle because they were not priests. So Phinehas began explaining about the fine linen woven with colors and the embroidered cherubim.

One boy interrupted, saying, "Oh, I know. My mother helped make that curtain. She did some of the spinning and weaving. She even helped to embroider the cherubim." The rest of the group looked at him with admiration. The boys knew that God had sought willing-hearted women. He gave them the ability to make the coverings and the curtains of the Tabernacle. (See Exodus 35:25-29.) Some who were particularly skillful made the curtains with the cherubim. The boy spoke softly, "Imagine that! My mother helped to make the curtain hanging inside the Holy Place." His eyes sparkled as he tried to imagine what it looked like.

Someone broke the silence. "What is it like on the other side of the veil?"

Phinehas explained, "The room behind the veil is *the Holy of Holies* or *the Most Holy Place*." Then, shaking his head, he said, "But I do not know what it is like. You see, even my father cannot go in there." The boys looked surprised. Phinehas continued, "Only the high priest may enter the Holy of Holies and he may go in only once a year. But my grandfather Aaron is the high priest. Someday he will tell me about that room."

Then Phinehas whispered, "When Grandfather Aaron dies, my father will become the high priest." There was a long silence. When Phinehas spoke again, it was even more softly. "And when my father dies, I shall be the high priest." The boys were quiet for a long time. It was such a serious thing! Yet somehow it was quite wonderful.

2. THE TABLE OF SHOWBREAD
Exodus 25:23-30; 37:10-16; John 6:35

But even serious-minded boys cannot remain quiet long. "Tell us more about the first room–the Holy Place. Your father knows what is in there."

Show Illustration #6

"On the north side (to their right when the priests enter) is the table of *showbread*."

"What is it made of?" one boy demanded. "What does it look like?"

"The table of showbread is made of wood covered with gold. It has a golden border–something like a crown–around the top edge. It is called the table of showbread because every Sabbath there are 12 loaves of bread placed on the table."

"Do the 12 loaves of bread stand for our 12 tribes?" someone wanted to know.

"Yes, they do," Phinehas replied.

"What happens to the old bread when fresh bread is put there?"

"It is food for the priests. Right there in the Holy Place they eat the bread that is taken from the table."

We must stop for a minute to talk about the likeness of the showbread to the Lord Jesus. This is perfectly clear. Jesus Himself said, "I am the bread of life; he who comes to Me will never hunger" (John 6:35). And, "If any many eat of this bread, he will live forever" (John 6:51).

In making bread, the wheat must first be crushed and ground into flour. Then it must be beaten together with the other ingredients and pierced with a sharp fork. Finally it goes into the heated oven. Surely these things remind us of the suffering of our Lord Jesus. Do you remember how He was lashed? (*Teacher:* You may go into more detail, if you desire.)

Jesus is the bread of God who came down from Heaven. (See John 6:33.) As we keep learning more of Him, reading God's Word and living for Him, we are "feeding on Him" as the priests fed on the showbread. (Remember, we too, are priests!)

3. THE LAMPSTAND
Exodus 25:31-39; 37:17-24; John 8:12

"What else is in the Holy Place?" another boy asked.

Show Illustration #7

"As you know, there are no windows in the Tabernacle but there is a light in the Holy Place. On the south side (to the left of the priests as they enter) is the solid gold lampstand." Lowering his voice, Phinehas added, "It is very valuable. My father says it is worth a talent of gold." (If Phinehas had been speaking in our time, he would have said "$145,600," instead of "a talent of gold." For that is about what a talent of gold would be worth today. No wonder the boys' eyes grew big!)

"It is a magnificent lampstand," Phinehas explained. "It's made of pure beaten gold and has beautiful carvings of flowers and branches. Seven little almond-shaped cups–one on each branch–hold the oil. Little flames burn in each cup. The light is never allowed to go out. It burns in the Holy Place day and night."

Does the lampstand remind you of the Lord Jesus Christ? The pure solid gold of the lampstand brings to mind that He is God the Son. It is made of beaten gold, which speaks of His sufferings. He is the light of the world–a light that is always shining. The Lord Jesus said, "He who follows Me will not walk in darkness but will have the light of life" (John 8:12).

4. THE ALTAR OF INCENSE
Exodus 30:1-8; 25-28; Hebrews 7:25

Phinehas explained, "There is one other piece of furniture in the Holy Place. It is the *golden altar* or the *altar of incense*."

Phinehas saw the boys look toward the brazen altar. He shook his head. "Oh, no!" he exclaimed. "The altar of incense is not at all like the brazen altar."

Show Illustration #8

He continued, "It is much smaller." (*Teacher:* It was only 18 inches square by 3 feet high. Compare its size with something your students know.) "Animal sacrifices are not burned on the golden altar only sweet-smelling incense. My father says there is always a sweet fragrance in the Holy Place for the incense burns all the time. The burning coals on this altar came from the brazen altar."

"Is the altar of incense made of solid gold?" someone asked.

"No, the altar is made of wood and covered with gold," Phinehas explained. "It also has a border around the top like a crown–just as the showbread table has."

It is not hard for you to understand this likeness of the Lord Jesus. The gold-covered wood tells us that the Lord Jesus is both God and man. But the crown is a reminder that one day He will be crowned King of kings.

The next likeness will not be hard for you to understand either–if you listen carefully. Several places in the Bible, prayer is spoken of as *incense*. Once it says, "Let my prayer be set before You [God] as incense" (Psalm 141:2). So the sweet-smelling incense is a reminder of the prayers of the Lord Jesus. "He ever lives to make intercession" for us. (See Hebrews 7:25.) To "make intercession" means *to pray*. Just as the incense burned continually in the Holy Place, so the Lord Jesus prays continually for those who belong to Him. He knows all the hard things that come into your life. He knows about each temptation. Because He is always praying for you, you do not have to yield to temptation. Did you ever promise to pray for someone–and then forget? He *never* forgets to pray for you!

The sweet-smelling spices on the incense altar had to be beaten and burned to bring out the fragrance. The coals from the brazen altar in the court were used to light the fire on the golden altar. The brazen altar tells of His death, His sacrifice. Just so, the Lord Jesus had to be our *suffering* Saviour before He could be our *praying* Saviour.

He died as your sacrifice. Have you ever received Him who gave His life for your sins? If not, will you do so right now?

Show Illustration #9

In our lesson today we have had three reminders of the Lord Jesus. Let us think about them again:

1. The table of showbread helps us to remember that He is the Bread of Life.
2. The lampstand reminds us that He is the Light of the World.
3. The altar of incense suggests that He who lives forever is praying for us.

These are wonderful truths if you have trusted the Lord Jesus. If you have not, they do not mean very much to you. Would you like to place your trust in Him today? (*Teacher:* Make invitation clear and plain.)

Lesson 3
THE MOST HOLY PLACE

Scripture to be studied: Exodus 16:32-34; 25:10-22; 37:1-9; Leviticus 16:1-22; Numbers 17:1-10; Deuteronomy 10:2, 5; Hebrews 9:4, 7-15; 10:1-14, 19-22

The *aim* of the lesson: That students may learn of the meeting place between God, the holy One, and sinful man.

What your students should *know*: That none can approach God except through a blood sacrifice for sin.

What your students should *feel*: A sense of sinfulness; gratitude for forgiveness of sin through the blood of Christ.

What your students should *do*:
Unsaved: Place their trust in the Saviour who cleanses from sin.
Saved: Determine to share the news of salvation with one particular friend this week.

Lesson outline for the teacher's and students' notebooks:
1. The Ark of the Covenant (Exodus 25:10-22; 37:1-9).
2. Inside the Ark of the Covenant (Exodus 16:32-34; Numbers 17:1-10; Deuteronomy 10:2, 5; Hebrews 9:4).
3. The Day of Atonement (Leviticus 16:1-22).
4. The Lord Jesus Christ and our Day of Atonement (Hebrews 9:7-15; 10:1-14, 19-22).

The verse to be memorized:

For Christ is not entered into the holy places made with hands, which are the figures of the true; but into Heaven itself, now to appear in the presence of God for us. (Hebrews 9:24)

NOTE TO THE TEACHER

Rehearse with your students the major types which have been presented thus far in the Tabernacle study. Remember this important law of teaching: review, review, review!

When you come to the close of the lesson, explain (if possible) that the Temple at Jerusalem replaced the Tabernacle in the wilderness. The veil that was torn when Christ died was not in the Tabernacle. It was in the Temple which contained the same kind of furnishings as the Tabernacle. (See 2 Chronicles 3:11-5:14.)

THE LESSON

Phinehas had been awaiting this day for a long time. Grandfather Aaron, the high priest, was coming to Phinehas's tent. His grandfather would answer his questions about the Tabernacle. Phinehas knew that the brazen altar and the laver were in the court. He remembered what the Tabernacle coverings were made of. He could tell what was in the Holy Place. But Phinehas did not know what was on the other side of the veil in the Most Holy Place–*the Holy of Holies*. His grandfather could tell him about this.

Almost as soon as Aaron arrived, Phinehas asked, "Grandfather, what's it like in the Most Holy Place?"

Grandfather Aaron smiled. As he spoke, his voice was soft and reverent. "There is no lamp, no candle, no window in the Most Holy Place. Yet it is not dark there. For an unusual kind of light fills the place. The light is from God Himself. It is a sign that He is with us."

Phinehas took a deep breath, but he did not interrupt.

1. THE ARK OF THE COVENANT
Exodus 25:10-22; 37:1-9

Show Illustration #10

Grandfather Aaron continued, "In the Holy of Holies there is one piece of furniture but it is in two parts. The bottom part is called the *Ark of the Covenant*. (Covenant means "agreement.") It is really a box made of wood, covered with gold. (*Teacher:* It was almost four feet long and a little over two feet wide and a bit more than two feet high. Compare with something of like size that your students may be able to see.)

"The top part–made of solid gold–is called the *Mercy Seat*. It is like a lid for the box. It is extremely beautiful. On each end of the Mercy Seat is a solid gold cherub. The two cherubim face each other. Their wings are stretched toward one another. Phinehas, this is the most special part of the whole Tabernacle."

"Why, Grandfather?"

Aaron replied, "God told Moses how the Mercy Seat should be made. At that time He promised, 'I shall meet with you from above the Mercy Seat, from between the two cherubim.' This is the spot where the glory of God's presence rests. That is why this part of the Tabernacle is the most wonderful of all, Phinehas."

2. INSIDE THE ARK OF THE COVENANT
Exodus 16:32-34; Numbers 17:1-10; Deuteronomy 10:2, 5; Hebrews 9:4

Show Illustration #11

Grandfather Aaron continued, "Inside the Ark of the Covenant are the tablets of stone bearing the Ten Commandments. There is also a pot of gold containing manna." (Why do you think God commanded His people to keep manna in the Ark of the Covenant? See Exodus 16:32.) When Aaron told all this to Phinehas he did not know that later on something else would be placed in the Ark of the Covenant.

Aaron did not know then. But *you* can know, if you listen carefully. Sometime after this, certain Israelite men were displeased because only Aaron and his family were priests. "We are just as good as Aaron," they insisted proudly.

So God instructed Moses, "Have a man from each tribe bring a rod. Tell each owner to write his name on his rod. Lay the rods in the Holy Place before the veil. Tomorrow morning one of the rods will have life in it. The owner of this rod–and the tribe he represents–will be My choice of those who are to serve Me."

The next morning Moses got the rods and took them out to the people. Immediately everyone saw that Aaron's rod was no longer a dead stick. It was alive. It had grown leaves and blossoms and almonds! God wanted His people to remember always that only those whom He had chosen were to serve Him. So He commanded that Aaron's rod be placed in the Ark of the Covenant along with the Ten Commandments and the pot of manna.

Are you ready for more reminders of the Lord Jesus?
1. In the Ark of the Covenant the gold and the wood remind us that Jesus Christ is both God and man.
2. He is the only One who perfectly obeyed God's holy law, the Ten Commandments.
3. He is the Bread–the manna–which came down from Heaven.
4. He is the resurrection and the life, as shown in the rod that came to life.

3. THE DAY OF ATONEMENT
Leviticus 16:1-22

Now, back to Phinehas. "I know, Grandfather," he began, "that you go into the Holy of Holies only once a year on our Day of Atonement. Will you please tell me more about it?"

"The Day of Atonement is the most solemn day of our whole year," Aaron explained. "It is a day of sorrow and sadness because of sin. It is the day when I, the high priest, meet with God for all the people of Israel. On this day I do not wear the beautiful robes of the high priest. I wear only plain linen clothes."

(Phinehas had always admired his grandfather's beautiful robes. Sometime he would ask about them. Right now he was interested in the Day of Atonement.)

The high priest told his grandson, "First of all, we kill a young bull at the brazen altar. I catch its blood in a basin and take it into the Holy Place. There, from the golden altar, I fill a censer with burning coals and incense."

Show Illustration #12

He continued, "As I enter the Holy of Holies, the smoke from the burning incense covers the Mercy Seat. (See Leviticus 16:12-13.) I dip my fingers into the blood in the basin and sprinkle it once upon the Mercy Seat. Again, I dip my fingers into the blood. This time I sprinkle it upon the earth in front of the Mercy Seat. Once . . . twice . . . three times, four, five, six, seven times in all, I sprinkle blood on the earth. The people are waiting on the outside of the Tabernacle. When I return, they know that because I obeyed the Lord, He accepted my offering. If I had not taken the kind of offering God asked for, He would have killed me. This first offering is for me and for those who live in my house. Next, I make an offering for the people.

"This time a goat is killed for the sins of the people," Grandfather Aaron explained. "Its blood is also caught in a basin. I take that blood through the veil into the Most Holy Place. I sprinkle the blood once on the Mercy Seat and seven times upon the earth."

4. THE LORD JESUS CHRIST AND OUR DAY OF ATONEMENT
Hebrews 9:7-15; 10:1-14; 19-22

While Phinehas is thinking about this special Day of Atonement, we want to think about the Lord Jesus.

Show Illustration #13

Sprinkling the blood once on the Mercy Seat reminds us that Jesus Christ died *once* for sin. In the Bible, the number seven is often used to show that something is perfect or complete. Sprinkling the blood seven times tells us that God took care of sin perfectly and completely.

The blood on the Mercy Seat satisfied God regarding the sins of the people. First, it satisfied Him because the people had obeyed Him by doing what He had asked them to do. Second, God was satisfied because the blood on the Mercy Seat pointed to what the Lord Jesus was going to do hundreds of years later.

Grandfather Aaron had one more thing to say. "When I return the second time from the Holy of Holies, the people know that God has accepted the sacrificial offering for their sin. Then I place my hands upon the head of a live goat and confess the sins of the people. This goat is sent away and deliberately lost in the wilderness forever. Our sins have been covered and forgotten. How glad we are for this great Day of Atonement!"

Again, we want to learn some things about our blessed Lord. Did you know that He is our High Priest? Did you know that *we* have a day of atonement? The Bible tells about these matters in the book of Hebrews.

On the Day of Atonement the high priest entered into the presence of God in the Most Holy Place. He took with him the blood of an animal for the sins of the people. Just so, the Lord Jesus (our great High Priest) has entered the presence of God–into Heaven itself. But the blood He gave was not that of animals. It was His own precious blood. He offered it for *your* sins and mine. It was *one* offering for *all* forever.

Now we do not need a yearly day of atonement. Our day of atonement occurred once. It is never to be repeated. When the Lord Jesus was crucified, He paid for our sins with His life, His blood. That was our day of atonement.

When Christ died, something amazing happened. In the Temple at Jerusalem, the massive veil between the Holy Place and the Holy of Holies was ripped apart all the way from the top to the bottom. (*Not* from the bottom to the top!) It was as if unseen hands had done it. And they had! *God* had torn that great veil. Because the Lord Jesus gave His blood, the way to God was forever open to every person who would receive Him.

When Jesus (the Lamb of God) died, the work of Aaron, Eleazar, Phinehas, plus the work of many other priests–was done. After the death of the Lord Jesus, God would never again accept an animal sacrifice. He would accept only the sacrifice of His Son. Have you received this sacrifice for your sin? No other will do. (*Teacher:* Give a clear, definite invitation.)

If you are already in the family of God, think of someone whom you would like to introduce to the Lord Jesus this week. Write that name in your notebook. Let's pray together that God will give you the opportunity to tell him of the Saviour.

Lesson 4
THE HIGH PRIEST

NOTE TO THE TEACHER
In your review, discuss the meanings of the contents of the Ark of the Covenant. Mention the activities of the high priest on the Day of Atonement. Be sure your students understand our day of atonement and who our High Priest is. Review, too, the torn veil. Since this will be your last lesson on the Tabernacle, take time to see that the message has reached the hearts of the students.

Scripture to be studied: Exodus 28:1-43; 39:1-31; Leviticus 8:6-9; Hebrews 2:9; 5:1-10; 6:13-20; 7:23-28; 8:1-6; 9:1–10:22

The *aim* of the lesson: To show that the Old Testament high priests are no longer needed because Christ is the Great High Priest.

What your students should *know*: The only way to come to God is through the Lord Jesus Christ.

What your students should *feel*: A desire to share the message of salvation to those who are trying to come to God some other way.

What your students should *do*: Plan to use their illustrations of the Tabernacle furnishings to introduce others to the Saviour.

Lesson outline for the teacher's and students' notebooks:
1. The garments of the High Priest (Exodus 28:1-14, 31-35, 39-43; 39:1-7, 22-29; Leviticus 8:6-7).
2. The breastplate and turban (Exodus 28:15-30, 36-38; 39:8-21, 30-31; Leviticus 8:8-9).
3. The Lord Jesus–our High Priest (Philippians 2:5-9; Hebrews 2:9; 5:1-10; 6:13-20; 7:23-28; 8:1-6).
4. The entire Tabernacle–a reminder of the Lord Jesus (Hebrews 9:1–10:22).

The verse to be memorized:
I am the way, the truth, and the life: no man cometh unto the Father, but by Me. (John 14:6)

THE LESSON

Phinehas was thrilled to see the priests doing their work at the Tabernacle each day. Each man knew what to do and when to do it. All were clothed in white linen from head to toe.

The Bible says that white linen is a symbol of righteousness. (See Revelation 19:8.) We are clothed in God's righteousness and serve as priests (Revelation 1:5-6; 5:9-10).

1. THE GARMENTS OF THE HIGH PRIEST
Exodus 28:1-14, 31-35, 39-43; 39:1-7, 22-29; Leviticus 8:6-7

Show Illustration #14
At first, Grandfather was dressed like all the priests: a white linen robe. But obeying God's command, Moses placed a long blue robe over Aaron's white one. Golden bells hung from the bottom of the robe. Between the bells were pomegranates. (A pomegranate is a fruit which looks something like an apple. Inside it is filled with hundreds of seeds.) Over the blue robe Moses placed a shorter one without sleeves. It was called an ephod. The beautiful linen material in the ephod was woven with blue, purple, scarlet and fine hammered gold thread. It was fastened on the shoulders by large onyx stones. (Onyx stones are precious gems.) On each stone the names of six of the tribes of Israel were engraved. So the high priest wore the names of the 12 tribes on his two shoulders.

2. THE BREASTPLATE AND TURBAN
Exodus 28:15-30, 36-38; 39:8-21, 30-31; Leviticus 8:8-9

Show Illustration #15
The ephod had a belt made of the same beautiful material. Moses then fastened a breastplate over Aaron's chest. The breastplate was held in place with golden chains and laces of blue. In the breastplate were 12 precious stones: an emerald, a sapphire, a diamond, an amethyst . . . and other beautiful gems. All were set in gold. On each of the 12 jewels was engraved the

– 28 –

name of one of the 12 tribes. The high priest not only had the names of the tribes of Israel on his shoulders, but also carried them near his heart.

Finally Moses placed a turban on Aaron's head. The turban had a gold plate in front. Phinehas could see writing on the plate. Looking closely, he saw the words "Holiness unto the Lord." Moses explained, "God said these garments are to be for glory and for beauty."

Phinehas, however, wanted his grandfather to tell him more about the special clothes of the high priest. "Do those bells and fruit around the bottom of the robe have some meaning, Grandfather?" he asked.

"Yes, my boy, they do. The bells ring as I walk about. When the people hear the bells, they are reminded of the Lord God. They know I am doing His work. And the bells speak to them of Him. But if the bells stopped tinkling, the people would know I had been struck dead for failing to approach the Lord in His appointed way!"

Grandfather Aaron continued, "The pomegranates remind me that I have been chosen to serve the Lord. The results of my service are as fruit to Him. We do not wear bells to cause people to think about the Lord. We remind them of Him by the things we say and by the way we live. The bells tell of our witness for Him. God also wants us to be fruit-bearing Christians. We do not wear pomegranates. But by living close to the Lord Jesus and witnessing to others, we are bearing fruit for Him.

"Why are the names of the tribes of Israel on the gems on your shoulders and on the breastplate?" Phinehas asked.

Grandfather Aaron heaved a big sigh. "I am very responsible for the children of Israel," he explained. "As their high priest, I stand between them and God. The shoulder is the place of strength. The names on my shoulders mean that I want to carry them through the hard places. I talk to God about them in prayer. I never forget that they're my responsibility. Their names in the jewels of the breastplate remind me that I hold them near my heart. The heart is the place of love." Again, Grandfather sighed, then smiled. "I do love my people very much," he added.

3. THE LORD JESUS, OUR HIGH PRIEST
Philippians 2:5-9; Hebrews 2:9; 5:1-10; 6:13-20; 7:23-28; 8:1-6

Show Illustration #16

Here is a splendid likeness of the Lord Jesus. He is the Strong One, crowned with glory and honor. (See Hebrews 2:9.) If you have received Him as your Saviour, He–the Lord of glory–carries you through the hard places. He upholds you on His shoulder–the place of strength. He also has you near His heart–because He loves you very much. What a wonderful High Priest He is!

Phinehas did not have to ask about the beautiful material in the ephod. He had already learned the meaning of the colors from the curtains of the Tabernacle. He understood why God said these garments were to be for glory and beauty. The high priest wore them every day but one–the Day of Atonement. Then, when he took the blood before the Lord God for the sins of all the people, he wore the plain white robe.

This, too, is a reminder of the Lord Jesus. When He lived in Heaven before coming to earth, He was clothed in majesty and glory. He, God the Son, was lifted above every angel in Heaven. But when He came to take our sins upon Himself, He laid aside that glory, just as the high priest laid aside His beautiful clothing on the Day of Atonement. After Christ died for our sins, He arose from the grave. Now He is in Heaven. And the glory, which had belonged to Him before He humbled Himself and came down to earth, is restored to Him! (See Philippians 2:5-9.)

Phinehas thought again about the time Moses had dressed his Grandfather Aaron in the high priest's garments. What a glorious day that had been! It was the day when the Tabernacle had first been set up. Thousands and thousands of men and women, boys and girls were there. The curtains had been put together, the pillars set up and the altar set in place. Then, when everything was completed, God's glory cloud filled the Tabernacle. No person could enter the Tabernacle–not even Moses or the high priest, as long as the cloud filled the building. For it was God, Himself, filling the whole place. Finally, the cloud lifted and rested above the Holy of Holies. There it stayed as a sign that God was present with His people. Phinehas knew he would never forget that day.

There have been many things for you to learn about the Tabernacle–this wonderful, movable tent. We hope that you, like Phinehas, will never forget. You have not seen the building, nor taken part in this worship as Phinehas did. So it will be harder for you to remember. But ask God to remind you of these lessons and the truths you have learned.

4. THE ENTIRE TABERNACLE: A REMINDER OF THE LORD JESUS
Hebrews 9:1–10:22

Show Illustration #17

(*Teacher:* Hold sideways with illustration #17 at top. Point to each furnishing as you mention it.) We have learned that the Lord Jesus alone is the *door*. The *brazen altar* reminds us that He is our sacrifice for sin. His blood is sufficient for past sins, present sins and even sins of the future! We come to Him once for the forgiveness of the penalty of sin. At that moment we become His child. The *laver* reminds us that those who have trusted in Christ must come to Him daily for cleansing. (See John 13:6-10; Ephesians 5:25-27.)

The *altar of incense* is a reminder that the Lord Jesus is praying for us. We remember Him as our Great High Priest when we think of the *Ark of the Covenant* and the *Mercy Seat*. He entered the very presence of God–not with the blood of animals, but with *His own precious blood* which He offered *once*. Because of His death and resurrection, all who trust in Him are set free from the penalty of sin forever.

(*Teacher:* For the conclusion, as you quote John 14:6, trace with your finger from the *gate* at the bottom to the *Mercy Seat* at the top, and from the *lampstand* to the *table of showbread*, emphasizing the shape of the cross.)

The Lord Jesus Christ is the one and only way to God. He said, "I am the way (point to *gate* and *brazen altar*), the truth and the life (point to *laver* and *altar of incense*): no one comes to the Father (point to *Ark* and *Mercy Seat*), but by Me" (point to *lampstand* and *table of showbread*). No one can ever approach God except through the blood of His Son, the Lord Jesus Christ. Have you placed all your trust in Him? If not, will you do so this moment?

If you are already His child, have you shared the truths of the Tabernacle with someone who doesn't know Him? Why not draw a large cross in your notebook and illustrate the furnishings. (*Teacher:* encourage students to sketch pages 17 and 18.) Then, use your notebook to tell family and friends the only way to come to God: through Christ, the Son of God, who gave His blood for their sins.

www.ingramcontent.com/pod-product-compliance
Lightning Source LLC
Chambersburg PA
CBHW060800090426
42736CB00002B/107